CU00762149

The Museum
of
Anatolian Civilizations

Edited By MELİH ARSLAN

in collaboration with
Okan CİNEMRE
Ülkü DEVECİOĞLU
M. Tevfik GÖKTÜRK
Mustafa METİN
Sena MUTLU
Mehmet SEVİM
Mehtap TÜRKMEN
Emel YURTTAGÜL
Candemir ZOROĞLU

A Guide to the Classical Ages
of Anatolia

With Thanks to:
Umut ALAGÖZ
Ertekin DOKSANALTI
Nejat GÜLŞEN
Haydar KAT
Erhan ÖZTEPE
Alptekin ORANSOY
Sevinaz GÜNAY
Güven SEVENCAN
Nihal TIRPAN

ISBN: 978-605-4745-82-1

Designed by Özlem ŞENTÜRKLÜ

Translation by Selim Ferruh ADALI

Photographs by Ahmet Remzi ERDOĞAN&Rasim KONYAR

Published by Alter Yay. Rek. Org.Tic. Ltd.Şti

Printing Office: Kalkan Matbaacılık San. ve Tic. Ltd. Şti.
Büyük Sanayi 1. Cad. Alibey İşhanı No: 99/32 Altındağ/ ANKARA
Certificate No: 16029

Front Cover: Bronze Head of a Bearded Man, Roman Period
Back Cover: Marble Head of a Young Athlete, Roman Period

Contents

A Guide to the Classical
Ages of Anatolia

Introduction:
The Classical Ages of Anatolia

The Classical Era Hall of the Museum of Anatolian Civilizations is open to visitors following the exhibition establishment project completed in 2013, in accordance with contemporary and scientific criteria. The artifacts are presented in 18 different display-cases with varying concepts and themes. The Hall boasts with a Museum collection of artifacts from the first millennium BC up to the Ottoman period (13th-19th centuries AD). These spectacular artifacts were acquired by the Museum of Anatolian Civilizations through purchase, donation, confiscation, as well as excavations and salvage operations. Each display-case of the Hall opens to a world of its own with its unique artifacts. Some basic information about these artifacts is provided herein.

Display Case 1: Relief and inscribed marble steles are displayed here under the title "Votive Steles". The steles displayed are 16 in number. Their naïve pictures reflect the rural culture of antiquity.

Some steles bear Greek inscriptions voicing the votive offerer's gratitude to Zeus Alsenos and Zeus Petarenos, while others depict organs such as the hand, arm, eye or ear; indicating which organ was healed after the votive offerer's appeal to the god. These votive steles reveal certain aspects of ancient rural culture.

The "Votive Steles" have been brought to the Museum's collection in 1964, gathered from the rural areas of Afyon, Emirdağ, the Village of Kurudere, and Kütahya. The Museum collection has 500 steles. Some of the steles were purchased by the Directorates of the Istanbul Archaeology Museums and the Kütahya Museum. A catalogue-book titled "Phrygian Votive Steles" includes all these artifacts; this book by Prof. Dr. Thomas Drew-Bear and his colleagues has been published by the Directorate of the Museum of Anatolian Civilizations in 1999 and can be purchased from our Museum store.

Display Case 2: Titled "Bronze Figurines", this display-case contains 42 artifacts. These are figurines of animals, human beings and goddesses ranging from the 6th century BC up to the 3rd century AD. There is the statuette of the seated goddess Cybele from the 6th century BC (no. 1). An artifact of Phrygian origin, it was used as a mould model. Among the most interesting artifacts, there is a Roman-period bronze Phalera with a depiction of Zeus (no. 16). Note also the statuette of Glykon, the human faced snake god (no. 22).

Display Case 3: Various types of containers, vessels and pieces of furniture dating from the 7th century BC up to the 10th century AD are displayed under "Metal Artifacts". Of these 30 artifacts of gold, silver or bronze, the gold framed silver bowl (no. 5) dates the earliest. The silver censer, dating to the 6th century BC, bears witness to the refinement of Lydian art. Omphalos (navel) bowls with reliefs, the silver ladle, the miniature jug, and the filtered pot are among the other very interesting artifacts in Display-Case III. No. 9 is a bronze cauldron appliqué in the form of a griffin's head. The two bronze jugs (Oenochoe, at no. 20) with handle tips in the form of the human head, and the handle of the bronze mirror with an animal protome are artifacts that date to the 7th and 6th centuries BC. The silver pyxis with a ram protome (no. 21) dates to the 6th century BC. The Roman-period bronze mirror (no. 15) with war reliefs on the reverse and the Byzantine-period silver bowl with a peacock relief tondo (no. 27) are noteworthy artifacts.

Display Case 4: "Lighting Luminaries Throughout the Ages" is the name of the display-case with a range of bronze, terracotta, and glass lamps dating from the 6th century BC up to the Seljuk period in the 12th century AD and thus showing very important evidence for the global human history of the luminaries.

The Museum collection includes Roman-period bronze lamps, from among which a swan-shaped lamp (no. 17), a lamp with a handle shaped as a horse's head (no. 18), and another lamp's handle like a lion's head (no. 19) draw attention, whereas the lamp holder (candelabrum) carried by the three greyhounds (no. 6) is a very significant work of lamp art and craft. The Museum's bronze lamp collection includes Byzantine-period samples with griffin, bird, fish and cross ornamentations, attesting to the brilliance of Byzantine bronze casting. Also worth seeing are the turquoise glazed ceramic lamps and the Roman period glass lamps (no. 33-34).

Display Case 5: "Glass Artifacts" includes a selection of the finest 40 artifacts from the Museum's very rich glass collection. The range of artifacts date from the 6th century BC up to the 15th century AD. The earliest ones are the alabastron and the amphoriskos vessels (no. 2-4) with Phoenician ornaments of coloured glass threads, dating to points of time between the 6th and 2nd centuries BC. The multi-coloured bowl (no. 5) dates Late Hellenistic/Early Roman. The cobalt blue glass phalera depicting the bust of child Germanicus (20-40 AD), brother of Roman Emperor Claudius (no. 29) is a rare and significant artifact. A less preserved sample is displayed in the British Museum. The feeding bottle (guttus, at no. 30) and the rhyton (no. 31) are noteworthy Roman-period artifacts.

Display Case 6: "Ancient Anatolian Jewelry" holds 139 very precious artifacts made of gold, silver, bronze, glass, precious and semi-precious stones. They date to periods between the 7th century BC and the 10th century AD, the Byzantine period. The highly refined taste of the ancient Anatolian woman and the high quality of jewelry making in Anatolia is evidenced in this display-case containing many different pieces of jewelry made of varying materials.

The gold amulet in the form of a bull-headed female figure (no. 39) dates to the 6th-5th centuries BC and was an object used for magic and

10

incantation. The silver armband (no. 23), the silver neck ring (torc, at no. 24), and the gold earrings with sardonyx stone and Eros depicted on the pendulum (no. 51-52) are among the finest and most refined samples of the Hellenistic period. From the Museum's rich jewelry collection, note also the fine workmanship of the Roman-period gold plated bronze mirror with the figure of Eros (no. 20), the gold necklace with its wheel-disc shaped clip (no. 22), the gold necklace pendulum and chain with a sardonyx stone cameo depicting an empress (3rd century AD) bust (no. 41); the necklace pendulum with a sardonyx stone depicting Medusa's head and a woven necklace chain (no. 44), and the gold brooch with a sardonyx stone cameo depicting, possibly, the head of a Roman emperor (no. 55).

The silver relic container (reliquary), into which sacred Christian objects were placed in the past, is covered with the reliefs of Jesus Christ and the Saints (no. 58). It is of great significance among the Byzantine period artifacts.

Display Case 7: "Ancient Gems and Rings" brings together 146 artifacts from the Museum's very rich collection of gem collections (of approximately 1500). Gold, silver, iron rings dating from the 5th century BC to the 5th century AD were mounted with precious or semi-precious ring stones that were engraved (intaglio) or carved (cameo). They were aesthetically pleasing ornaments but the ring stones primarily served as the personal seal of its owner, used to mark somebody's property, express his/her authority, and to certify the private ownership of certain objects. Furthermore, there is some evidence that precious and semi-precious stones were used in superstitious contexts. It was believed that some stones had healing and apotropaic magical powers. For example, it was believed that a kind of agate stone protected against spider bites and scorpion venom. Hematite stone was good for the eyes and the liver. Amethyst stone expelled drunkenness. The Roman period witnessed a surge in the use of stones for magical purposes.

Precious carved stones could serve as love charms, sometimes to gain the attention of a disinterested lover, sometimes to take revenge against a cheating spouse.

I would like to draw your attention to some of the rings and crafted stones in this display-case. The gold ring depicting Persephone standing and the partridge (no. 1) dates to the 5th century BC. Dating to the 1st century BC is the gold ring (no. 2) with carnelian stone, depicting the head of Diadumenos. A red jasper ring stone (no. 5) depicts Mount Erciyes and the Legion Eagle. Harpokrates is depicted on a green chalcedony ring stone (no. 14). The busts of the emperor and the empress face each other on a large amethyst ring stone (no. 16). Nymphe's head appears on a green jasper ring stone (no. 22). A red jasper ring stone shows the empress (no. 37). A rock crystal ring stone (no. 44) depicts a pheasant. The ring stone depicting a lion and the moon with star is astrological (no. 45). The moon and star also appear on a carnelian ring stone (no. 48). One ring stone shows the battle between Bellerophon and the Chimera (no. 50). An ant appears on a carnelian ring stone (no. 71). The two tips of a silver ring are shaped as a dog's head (no. 78).

Display Case 8: "Islamic Coins" is where 58 select coins of different Islamic and Turkish states are exhibited. They date to different periods between the 7th and 19th centuries AD. Gold, silver and bronze coins as well as Ottoman "Orders of Merit" (Liyakat Nişanları) and other medals are exhibited in this display-case.

Display Case 9: 66 coins are at display at "Byzantine Coins", dating to different periods between the 4th and 15th centuries AD. Minted under the patronage of Byzantine emperors, these coins were gold, electrum, silver and bronze.

Display Case 10: "Roman Coins" is the display-case for 186 coins of Anatolian cities from the periods of the Roman Republic and the Roman Empire. The oldest of the gold, silver, and bronze coins date to the Roman Republic period, between the 2nd century BC and the 1st century AD (no. 1-9). The life-like portraits of the Roman emperors and empresses begin with the coin of Augustus (27 BC-14 AD) at no. 10 and end with the coin of Honorius (393-423 AD) at no. 112.

The semi-autonomous cities of Asia Minor minted bronze coins (no. 113-186). The obverse portrays the emperor in power. The reverse depicts the city's temple or chief god/goddess worshipped along with the name of the city in Greek.

The commemorative coins (no. 183-186) are medal-like. No. 183 was minted at Mysia-Pergamon during the time of Caracalla (198-217 AD). The reverse of the coin depicts the three Neokoros temples built in the name of the Emperor. The rare honour of building three temples in the name of the emperor was given to few cities such as Ephesus, Smyrna and Pergamon. Pergamon put the three Neokoros temples on her coins for propaganda. The obverse of another medal-like coin, no. 184, contains the portrait of Antinous (d. 132 AD). This young man Antinous was a favourite of Roman Emperor Hadrianus. In 132 AD, Antinous drowned in the Nile and was deified by Emperor Hadrianus, even cities were built in his name. This young man was from Bithynia-Claudiopolis (Bolu). After his demise, many cities in Asia Minor minted coins and medals in the name of deified Antinous. No. 185 is a bronze medal from the city of Perinthus at Thrace, minted during the reign of Caracalla. Depicted on this coin is one of the "twelve labours" of Herakles, his capture of Artemis's sacred deer of Keryneia. Herakles was regarded as the founder of the city of Perinthus, hence his name often appears on the city coins as the founder-hero (ktistes). The city's name appears as Herakleia, following the name of Herakles, during the Hellenistic period and the subsequent Byzantine period. Medal no. 186 has on the obverse a beautiful portrait of Emperor Trebonianus Gallus (251-253 AD) whereas the reverse depicts Victoria, the winged goddess of victory, leading the way back to Rome having won a victory

(ADVENTVS), with the emperor on horseback accompanied by his close circle.

Display Case 11: 99 coins dating between the 7th/6th centuries BC and the 1st century BC are on display at "Greek Coins". The gold, electrum, silver and bronze coins belong to various kings and city-states. No. 50 contains electrum coins minted from natural gold by the inventors of coinage, the Lydian Kingdom. The Lydian coat of arms, the lion with open jaws, appears on the obverse of these coins. The reverse contains the irregular square incuse. A gold stater (no. 9) depicts Darius the Persian king running. The lion, Satyr, and fish appear on the electrum coins (no. 31-32) of Mysia-Kyzikos (500-450 BC), which are also among the early dating coins worth seeing. The obverse of a silver tetradrachmi (no. 7) depicts the bearded head of Poseidon the sea god. On the reverse, Apollon sits on the prow of the ship. Additionally, I would like to draw your attention to some of the rare and very well preserved coins of the Hellenistic Seleucid kings. No. 13 is an excavation find from Gordion, a rare gold octodrachmi of Antiokhos I (280-261 BC). The life-like portraits on this coin and on the gold octodrachmi of Seleukos III (226-223 BC) at no. 14 are definitely worth looking at, as in the very beautiful portrait of the child ruler Antiokhos (175-170 BC) found on a silver tetradrachmi (no. 30). The city mints in Asia Minor were also responsible for exquisite pieces. For example, see a silver drachmi from Sinope (no. 41), with Nymphe on the obverse and the reverse depicting the sea eagle that has caught a dolphin with its talon. This coins dates to the 4th century BC. A silver stater (450-386 BC) from the city of Kilikia-Soli depicts a grape bundle (no. 74).

Display Case 12 : "Greek and Roman Sculptural Artifacts" covers four different display-cases. The first two display-cases are claret red in background and they exhibit individual statues and statue heads. The display-case with the green background exhibits small or middle sized statues of Roman period gods and goddesses. Most of the sculptural artifacts are made from marble. There are 9 marble statue heads at "Display-Case XII". Persian type heads (no. 1-2) date to the 4th century BC and reflect the traces of the Achaemenid period in Asia Minor. No. 4 is a limestone woman's head found at the excavation of Kommagene – Samosata and probably belonged to a statue made of the Kommagene royal family member. No. 6 is a young man's head, it might have depicted a prince of the Julius Claudius dynasty. A woman's portrait found at Sinop (no. 8) is one of the most beautiful portraits known of Livia, the dear wife of Augustus, founder of the Roman Empire.

Display Case 13: This display-case boasts with very fine portraits of men and women. The statuettes of administrators (no. 1-2) and the foot-shaped statues (no. 10-11) are noteworthy. The human foot-shaped votive statues are often considered as parts of a larger statue but looking at the way they were made, one can argue that they are votive artifacts offered to the gods and the temple by someone praying for the healing of an illness or discomfort regarding the feet or by someone giving thanks for the realization of such healing. There is a vase (krater) on the obverse of the foot statuette (no. 10), surrounded by two griffins and a divine attribute represented by a bundle of thunderbolts above.

Display case 14: This display-case exhibits Roman period artifacts; 11 statuettes and 2 busts. Most of the god and goddess statuettes here were found in a stone hearth at the Village of Kutludüğün at Ankara-Kayaş in 1951. The majority are Asklepios and Hygieia statuettes. They must have been produced as votive artifacts for offering at the Asklepios Sotereia (Asklepios the Saviour) festivities held in ancient Ancyra. There is the bust of the sky god Men (no. 1), the deity wears a Phrygian cap and on his shoulder is a crescent. This bust was found in 1988, during a construction drill. This deity was the most beloved native god of ancient Ankara. The other bust in this display-case (no. 5) is that of

Zeus, dedicated to the cult of Zeus Olybrios. The inscription on this bust indicates that the votive offerer was a follower of the cult, a priest named Chillon.

Display Case 15: 15 artifacts of the Roman period are displayed here, of which 4 are middle sized statues and the rest small sized statuettes of deities and statuette heads. The Helios-Mithras Statue (no. 1) is significant. Helios bears the crown of light and has donned armour. He holds a spear in his right hand and a sword named parazonium in his left. The statuette of Hekate (no. 8), the three headed god of revenge, along with other evidence from sculptural artifacts and coins, indicates that this deity was worshipped in ancient Ankara.

Display Case 16: "Ceramic Pottery" boasts with 70 pieces of ceramic artifacts. The ceramic artifacts date to different periods between the 8th century BC and the 3rd century AD, with 40 of these artifacts dating to times between the 8th and 4th centuries BC. One of the oldest artifacts is a Fikellura style amphora with motifs of meander on its neck and lotus flowers on its shoulder (no. 1), produced in Miletos and dating to the 7th century BC. Cypriot Geometric style artifacts (no. 2-5) date to the 8th century BC. Red-figure Attika ceramics (no. 17-31), which date to the 5th century BC, were discovered in the 1940s during the Sinop Matchbox Factory Construction excavation. Among these, a scene of the musicians playing instruments at the Dionysos festivals can be found on a bell krater (no. 17). The grey-painted vessel in the form of an animal hide (no. 16) is a Phrygian artifact that dates to the 7th and 6th centuries BC.

Display Case 17: 30 artifacts are exhibited here. These artifacts date to different periods between the 4th century BC and the 3rd century AD. The Galatian pottery, produced locally in Anatolia, holds an important place among these artifacts. These ceramics date to the 3rd and 2nd centuries BC, among them the amphora (no. 7) and the oinochoe (no. 8) are typical Galatian pottery. Among the rare Hellenistic period artifacts is a black and red painted amphora with white slip (no. 6) discovered at the Kültepe excavations. The body of the amphora depicts a hunter on horseback holding a spear and hunting a wild animal (a leopard?). The Early Roman period double-handled deep cup (no. 22) has a relief with erotic scenes. The green glazed skyphos (no. 23) is one of the rare examples of Late Hellenistic/Early Roman period glazed ceramics. Red and black glazed plates (No. 24-26) were found in the Gordion excavations and date to the Early Roman period.

Display Case 18: "Terracotta Figures" has 52 artifacts selected with great care from the vast collection of the Museum, dating to times between the 2nd millennium BC and the 6th century AD. This exhibition comprises human and animal figures and architectural ornaments. The bull figures and heads (no. 3-5) date to the 2nd millennium BC and are the earliest and exceptional examples. Another early example was a statuette of a cow (no. 6) found at the Alacahöyük excavations. The Astarte statuettes (no. 14), of north Syrian origin, date to the 6th century BC and were figurines used for votive purposes. The architectural relief ornament of coloured Medusa (no. 1) dates to the 7th and 6th centuries BC. Women statuettes carrying a jug (Hydria) on their head (no. 15) and the bearded man statuettes wearing the polos are votive statuettes dating to the 5th century BC. The Aphrodite statuettes (no. 23-25) date to the Hellenistic period. The coloured Cybele statuette (no. 32), with the goddess sitting on her throne, dates to the 5th and 4th centuries BC. The latest dating artifact in this display-case is the woman's head (no. 28) dating to the 6th century AD, possibly meant as a depiction of a Byzantine empress.

Five sculptural artifacts are exhibited at the entrance of the Classical Era Hall. One is a tombstone in the shape of an Ionic capital, with a lion lying above it. The lower part of the tombstone contains a Greek inscription: "Mikos, son of Metrodoros". This limestone funerary stele dates to the 6ᵗʰ century BC and originates from the region of Caria. Another statue at the entrance of the Hall is the bronze statue of naked Dionysos, god of fertility and wine. This statue dates to the Roman period. It was smuggled out of Turkey. The efforts to repatriate the artifact bore fruit and it was returned to Turkey in 2003. A Roman period marble statue of Athena, the statuette of Hygenia and the funerary stele of Chrisampelos the Gladiator are at the Hall entrance, on the right. Furthermore, there are two limestone ostothecas (ostothek) at the entrance of the Hall, they are part of a group of artifacts dubbed the Pamphylia style of the Roman Imperial period. They have reliefs depicting garlands with Eros and Medusa's head.

Melih ARSLAN
April 2013

Plan of Exhibition

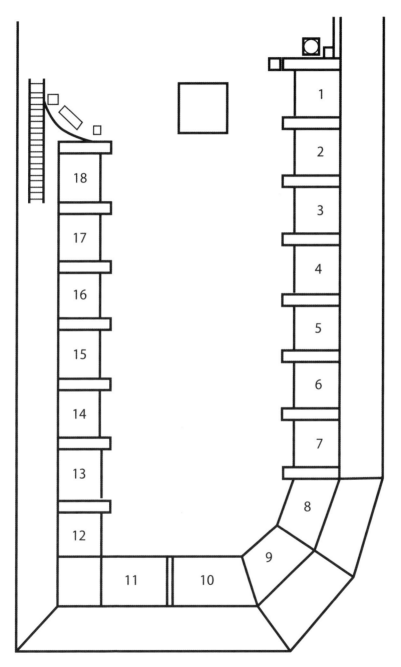

Plan of Exhibition

Votive Steles
From Phrygia,
Kütahya and Afyon

Since very early times people have offered votive objects to the gods or goddesses to give thanks or to express their wishes and prayers. Votive steles comprised most of these cult objects in Roman period Phrygia. Most of the votive steles in the Museum, acquired between 1964-1966, were found in the regions of Afyon and Kütahya.

Marble Votive Stele Relief of Zeus Thallos and Bulls

Aur(elios) Lykotes Son of Zenon (dedicates) this to Zeus Thallos

Steles were made by the members of local populace, dedicated to the local deities such as Zeus Alsenos, Zeus Petarenos, Zeus Ampelikos, Zeus Ampeleites and Zeus Thallos. Their epithets indicate the specific function of these local deities and hint at their protective roles. Zeus Thallos, for example, is "Zeus, protector of young olive-shoots", while Zeus Ampeleites and Zeus Ampelikos represent "Zeus, protector of vineyards", and Zeus Alsenos is "Zeus, protector of the groves". There are also titles of gods which indicate the provenance of the local cult as in the case of Zeus Petarenos.

...villager (dedicates) this to Zeus A(m)peleites

The people of the rural areas petitioned their gods in the face of their daily problems. They prayed especially concerning health problems. This is supported by the presence of the body parts (eyes, arms, legs, hands, breasts, etc.) carved on the steles. Additionally, the depiction of agricultural tools on votive steles expresses a wish for a fruitful harvest. Shepherds, dressed in peaked felt cloak, or pairs of ploughing animals, are depicted on some of the steles. Such imagery can be seen on votive objects that seek the health and safety of livestock.

Babeis (dedicated) this to Zeus Alsenos

Kasmeina (dedicated) this to Zeus Alsenos

Olympikos from the village of the Brianenoi, wow to Zeus Petarenos

Bronze Figure and Figurines

The techniques employed to produce bronze statues and smaller metal figurines were similiar. In ancient times, wooden, clay and wax moulds were used for casting the metal. Each mould could only be used once, and so every artifact was unique in some way. The casting of a large statue required a fully equipped workshop but this was not essential for making smaller figurines. As the demand for small bronzes increased, new smaller workshops opened in every region, except for the great cities with their more established studios. There were even traveling workshops. One of the fundamentals of statuette production was to make them cheap and affordable. To keep production costs as low as possible, the amount of metal used was minimized. This, rather than technical reasons, explains why figurines larger than 5 cm were mostly produced with hollow rather than solid castings. Religions and cults grew significantly due to various social movements within the expanding Roman Empire. The new cults gave rise to a demand for their particular symbols, that is the statuettes of deities, and the animal figurines that represented the divine attributes.

Mould Statuette with the Depiction of Seated Kybele, 6ᵗʰ Century BC

Serpent Statuette with Human Face (Glykon), Roman Period

Consequently, the smaller local and travelling workshops proliferated. The figurines they produced looked back to Classical and Hellenistic predecessors, but their products fell short in terms of quality. People preferred small bronzes because they were easy to carry.

Statuette of Deer, Roman Period

The faithful could take them anywhere and this provided individuals with a sense that they were accompanied by the gods. The great majority of the bronzes were associated with a specific cult. They could be taken to the altars of a cult's sacred precinct, but they also allowed those who were unable to visit the temples to conduct their worship at home or at work.

Statuette of Bull, Roman Period

Statuette of Aphrodite,
Roman Period

Statuette of Apollon,
Roman Period

Statuette of Hermes,
Roman Period

Statuette of Heracles,
Roman Period

Bearded Man's Head, Period of Antoninus Pius, AD 138 - 161

Finally, of course, the small, mass produced, low quality bronze figurines were preferred because they were affordable to more people, unlike the expensive items produced in famous and important centres.

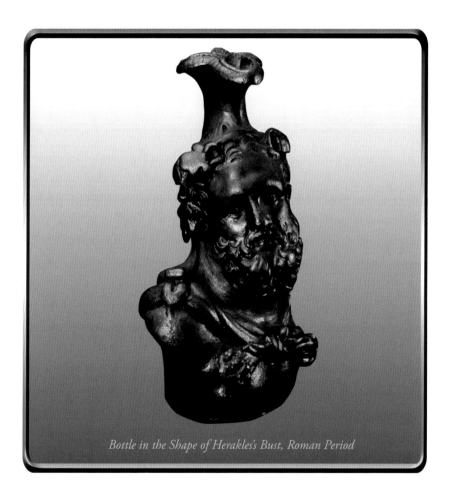

Bottle in the Shape of Herakles's Bust, Roman Period

Bronz Mobilya Aksamı (Fulcra), *Helenistik Dönem*
...vlcra) with Eros and Lion Relief, *Hellenistic Period*
...HÖ 6. Yüzyıl
...8° Century BC

10 Atlı Sapı Tasvirli Bronz Mobilya Aksamı (Fulcra), *Helenistik Dönem*
Bronze Furniture Piece Depicting a Horse's Head, *Hellenistic Period*

11 Bronz Fibulalar, *Roma Dönemi*
Bronze Fibulae, *Roman Period*

Bronz Fibula, *Roma Dönemi*

13 Bronz Fibula, *Roma Dönemi*
Bronze Fibula, *Roman Period*

14 Kurşun Ayna, *Roma Dönemi*
Lead Mirror, *Roman Period*

15 Kabartmalı Gümüş Ayna, *Roma Dönemi*
Silver Mirror with Relief, *Roman Period*

Saçlı Hayvan Protomlu Bronz Ayna, *HÖ 7. - 6. Yüzyıl*
16 Bronze Mirror with Animal Protome Handle, *7° - 6° Cent...*

17 Boğa Kabartmalı, Onylonelu Gümüş Kesı (Phiale), *U...*
Silver Bowl with Omphalos and Bull Relief (Phiale), *V...*

Gümüş Tek Kulplu ve Güngeli Sohluk, *Lidya Dönemi, V...*
18 Side-Spouted Silver Dish with Single Handle, *Lydian P...*

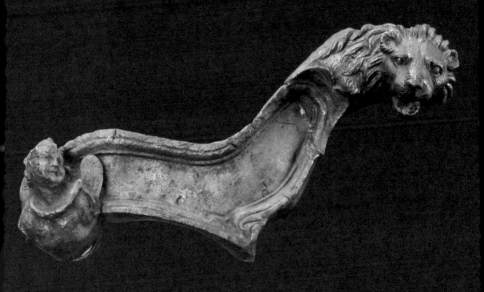

Metal Artifacts

Bronze is an alloy of various metals with copper. It is a hardened and durable metal, which is made by combining extremely soft copper, tin and lead. This metal has been used frequently for making of hand tools and large-sized statues.

The earliest bronze artifacts were used in the Chalcolithic period of Anatolia, Iran and Cyprus. At first its use was limited to metal wares, statues, reliefs, jewelry and military equipment such as arms and armour due to its scantiness. After the discovery of casting and deep mining techniques, bronze became more popular. Metal is reusable, so many metal objects were melted and the metal was reused for the production of other objects in antiquity and only a small portion of antique bronze objects produced are extant today.

Silver Bowl with Gold - Covered Rim (phiale)
Phrygian Period, 7ᵗʰ - 6ᵗʰ Centuries BC

Bronze Jugs with Human Head Protome Handles, 6ᵗʰ Century BC

Bronze Mirror, Handle with Animal Protome, 7th - 6th Centuries BC

The earliest metalworking method was the hammering technique. The most popular products of this technique were the shallow bowls and arms. The earliest known hammered bronze objects in the world were found in Çayönü (Diyarbakır) and date to the ninth millennium BC. Suitable also for mass production was the casting method, according to which the melted metal was poured into moulds, to make, for example, statuettes or small reliefs. The oldest known examples of this technique were found in Canhasan and date to the fifth millennium BC. Another method for producing metal bowls is the lathe turning technique, done by compressing metal plates into moulds. Incising, cutting, répousse and filigree techniques were used to decorate the surfaces of bronze objects.

Silver Miniature Jug, Lydian Period, 6ᵗʰ Century BC

Silver Pyxis with Ram Protome
Lydian Period, 5ᵗʰ Century BC

Bronze was a widely used material in ancient Greece and Rome. This material was also used for the cheap imitation artifacts of gold and bronze objects. In the beginning of the first millennium BC, the Greeks used this material both for religious objects and for the figurines and for the military equipment. In the Archaic period, the earliest life-sized bronze statues were cast and placed in agoras, temples and theaters. In the Classical period, decorated bronze vessels were produced besides statues, with scenes of Greek art and mythology. Improvements in mining technology brought about the wider and cheaper production of bronze artifacts in the Hellenistic period. Produced in great amounts, these richly ornamented bronze objects reflect Greek and oriental elements.

At the same period, bronze was widely used for the production of a wide range of tools and items such as pottery, medical instruments, jewellery and statuettes.

Silver Incense Burner,
Lydian Period, 6ᵗʰ Century BC

Silver Bowl with Omphalos and Bull Relief (Phiale),
Lydian Period, 6ᵗʰ Century BC

Bronze was also preferred in daily objects during Roman period and not just for artworks. There were numerous workshops, permanently based or travelling, that manufactured and sold bronze objects. In the first and second centuries AD, large-sized bronze statues of significant figures (emperors, commanders, statesmen) were manufactured along with little figurines.

Bronze Cauldron Applique with a Griffin's Head, 650-625 BC

Silver Mirror with Relief, Roman Period

The gods, gladiator statuettes, grotesque figures, and animals such as the lion, bull, and boar were very popular topics for Roman period statuettes. Pottery and oil lamps were as widespread as bronze made tools and items. Vessels were tinned and used for wine preparing and services. Bronze plates and furniture such as wooden boxes and klines (couches) were widely used in daily life.

19 Chakças amphora Kɾaɫɾ Bɩɩɩntɪ Pığmaɪ Yɑgɾɑlɪ Kɑndɪl. *Ronɑ Dönemı*
Terracotta Lamp with Amphora Krater in the Hanon. *Roman Period*

20 Kɑlɪp İbİlɪ Pığmaɪ Yɑgɾɑlɪ Kɑndɪl. *Ronɑ Dönemı*
Terracotta Lamp with Festive Nozzles. *Roman Period*

21 Kɑlɪp Biçimİ Bronz Kɑndɪl. *Ronɑ Dönemı*
Swan Shaped Bronze Lamp. *Roman Period*

22 Kulbu Al Bɑp Biçimİ Bronz Kɑndɪl. *Ronɑ Dönemı*
Bronze Lamp, Handle in the Shape of the Horse's head. *Roman Period*

21 Kulbu Sɑɾmɑşık Yɑgɾɑlɪ Biçimİ Bronz Kɑndɪl. *Ronɑ Dönemı*
Bronze Lamp, Handle in the Shape of Ivy Leaf. *Roman Period*

22 Kulbu Akɑnthus Yɑgɾɑlɪ Biçimİ Bronz Kɑndɪl. *Ronɑ Dönemı*
Bronze Lamp, Handle in the Shape of the Acanthus Leaf. *Roman Period*

Illumination Instruments
Antique Oil Lamps

The discovery of fire was the biggest step forward in civilization for mankind. After discovering that fire could generate heat and illuminate, mankind could easily invent the devices necessary in daily life. Fire lit in caves and huts not only generated heat but also enabled the cooking of more edible and tasty food, as well as providing protection against the attacks of wild animals by illuminating the surroundings. Tools inside of which a controlled fire could be lit were invented for times of day when the sun and moon provided only inadequate illumination. Besides simple solutions such as the torch or firewood, safer tools that better controlled fire were developed in time. The first lamps were seashells filled with animal or vegetable oil, paving the way in the future for terracotta oil lamps. Oil lamps are the oldest known tools of illumination; used in antiquity was votive objects in temples or as funerary offerings.

Terracotta Lamp with Three Nozzles, Roman Period

Terracotta Lamp with Triton and Fish in the Discus, Roman Period

Bronze Lamp with Hound Shaped Feet, Roman Period

Bronze Lamp, Handle in the Shape of the Lion's Head, Roman Period

Bronze Lamp with Handle in Mountain Goat Ornament, Roman Period

Footed Bronze Lamp, Byzantine Period

Suspending Bronze Lamp with Griffin-Bird-Fish and Cross Ornaments, Byzantine Period

Archaeological studies indicate that illumination tools were used around the Mediterrenean basin, in Syria, Palestine, Cyprus, Greece and Anatolia as early as the second millennium BC. These were terracotta bowls containing inside the oil and wick. The potter's wheel and moulding enabled the mass production of Hellenistic and Roman period oil lamps depicting historical figures, daily life, erotic, mythological or hunting scenes, seashells, animals, flowers and vegetal ornamentations.

Swan Shaped Bronze Lamp, Roman Period

Glass Lamp, Roman Period

In the Christian faith, "flame or light" (from the sun, candle or oil lamp) represented the eternal nature of Jesus, one with God, and of heaven. Various tools provided for illumination, from an architectural point of view, in daily life and especially during church rites and ceremonies. Such tools were attributed symbolic meaning according to their perceived attributes. The use of oil lamps continued into the Seljuk period, often made of terracotta or bronze.

Turquoise Glazed Terracotta Lamp, Seljukid Period

Glass in the
Ancient World

Glass is considered the first artificial material. It consists of silica, soda and limestone melted at around 1000 degrees Celcius. The oldest known samples of glass are glass beads discovered in Sumerian settlements dated to the first half of the third millennium BC.

The first glass vessels imitating ceramic samples appear in the mid-second millennium BC. These vessels were made according to the "Core Forming Technique", used for a very long time in glass making until the discovery of the blowing technique.

Forms made by means of the core forming technique, along with casting and cutting techniques, prevailed in the first millennium BC. Glass artists preferred to vessels using either transparent greenish or uncoloured glass imitating rock crystal, contrary to earlier traditions using opaque glass to imitate semi-precious stones.

Dark Blue Glass Alabastron, 6ᵗʰ-5ᵗʰ Centuries BC

Ribbon Glass Cup, 1ˢᵗ Century AD

Opaque Black, Blue, Red
Unguent Bottles (Amphoriskos)
2nd-1st Centuries BC

Unguent Bottles (Amphoriskos),
1ˢᵗ Century AD

More refined colourless glass bowls provide for the new forms in the fifth century BC, a time when there was more differentation between the casting and cutting techniques. These bowls were in the shape of metal vessels, mostly reminiscent of rock crystals. There were two regions that stood out in the production of glass in the Hellenistic period. One was Alexandria, capital of the Ptolemaic Kingdom of Egypt.

Green Glass Amphoriskos,
Roman Period

The other consisted of the settlements along the Syrian coast. The development of the casting (or sagging) technique accelerated the production of the vessels. Glass artifacts became part of daily life. The technique allowed for the production of ribbed and plain bowls as well as those made of mosaic glass, another type of vessel.

Large Roman Green Glass Rectanguler Flask
1ˢᵗ - 2ⁿᵈ Centuries AD

A Translucent Green Glass Double Balsamarium, Late Roman Period, 4ᵗʰ-5ᵗʰ Centuries AD

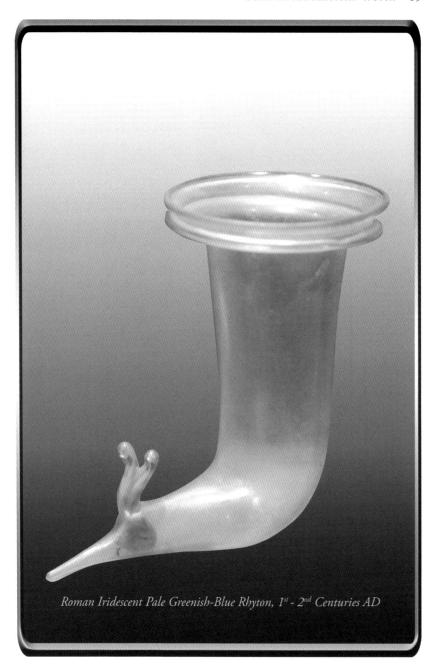

Roman Iridescent Pale Greenish-Blue Rhyton, 1ˢᵗ - 2ⁿᵈ Centuries AD

Glass Phalere with Bust of Germanicus,
First Quarter of the 1st Century AD

The blowpipe is the greatest invention in the history of glass. Excavations and current research accepts that the blowpipe was invented in the first century BC, in the Syria-Palestine region. The glass industry developed rapidly thanks to this invention and a diverse range of glass artifacts became an irreplaceable part of our daily lives.

Roman Blue Ribbed Glass Cup, 1st Century AD

Jug with Filter, Byzantine-Islamic Period

Ancient
Anatolian
Jewelry

Humanity's transition to sedentary life in the Neolithic Period brought about many cultural developments and changes. Doubtless one of the most important of these, before the development of pottery usage in human culture, was the making of personal ornaments from seashells, bones, stones and horn. These stone and organic-material ornaments were deposited as gifts in the graves of the deceased. Nevertheless, the true art of the jeweller was only born once humanity had mastered metal working, and when jewellery compositions predominantly involved the joint use of metal and stone, with precious stones functioning as seals. Metal artefacts uncovered at the sites of Troy, Alacahöyük and Eskiyapar are significant in shedding light on the developments and improvements in jewellery manufacture during the 3rd millennium BC. But it is in the 1st millennium BC that ancient jewellery's diversity is broadly manifested, by an increasingly substantial material record, and through descriptions in ancient written sources and visiual depictions in Classical vase paintings and statuary.

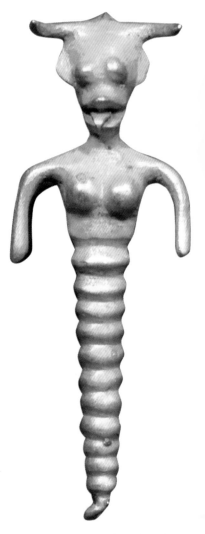

Composite Creature Shaped Gold Amulet,
6th - 5th Centuries BC

Silver Bracelet with Calf's Head Ornament,
Hellenistic Period

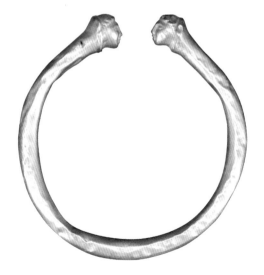

Gold Bracelet with Human's Head Ornament,
Hellenistic Period

*Gold Ring with Greeting Hand,
Roman Period*

The purpose of jewellery was similar from the Neolithic to the Roman Period, as today: primarily to beautify and complement clothing, to display wealth, and to catch the eye. The type and quantity of materials used were dependent on the owner's status and resources but gold has always been the most preferred metal. Jewellery items were commonly presented as gifts on special occasions such as births, birthdays and weddings. Some pieces of jewellery were handed down from one generation to the next, thereby increasing their value and significance.

Gold Ring with Depicting Athena, Classical Period 5th Century BC

Jewellery could also have a religious significance and could be intended to function as an amulet against evil, danger or disease. It was preferred by women in particular for making offerings to the gods. Such offerings were made in a variety of ways for different purposes. For example, pieces of jewellery were offered to Aphrodite during transitional stages in a woman's life, in order to express gratitude to the goddess for protecting her husband or lover, or in the hope of avoiding misfortune.

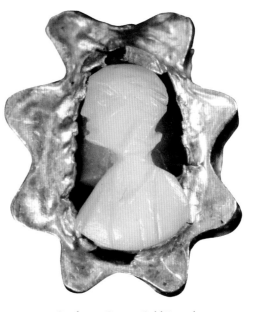

Sardonyx Cameo Gold Brooch,
Depicting the Empress, Roman Period

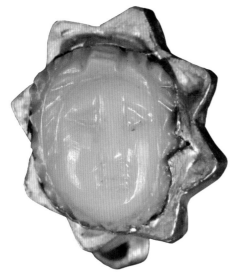

Similarly, patients made offerings to Asclepius in gratitude for restoring their health. Gifts made by women to win the love of a man are an entirely different type of offering to the gods. For example, Aspasia offered a "golden strigil" at the wooden altar of the Parthenon in order to win the heart of Pericles.

Sardonyx Cameo Gold Brooch, Depicting Eros,
Roman Period

Blue and Green Beaded Earing, Byzantine Period

Gold Ring with Double Coil and Stone, Roman Period

Blue Glass Beaded Necklace, Byzantine Period

*Gold Necklace with Bell-Shaped Pendulum, Ornamented with
Crimson Stone Beads, Roman Period*

*Necklace, Glass and Frit Beaded on Bronze Chain,
Hellenistic Period*

Sardonyx Cameo and Gold Necklace Chain with Empress,
Roman Period, 3rd Century AD

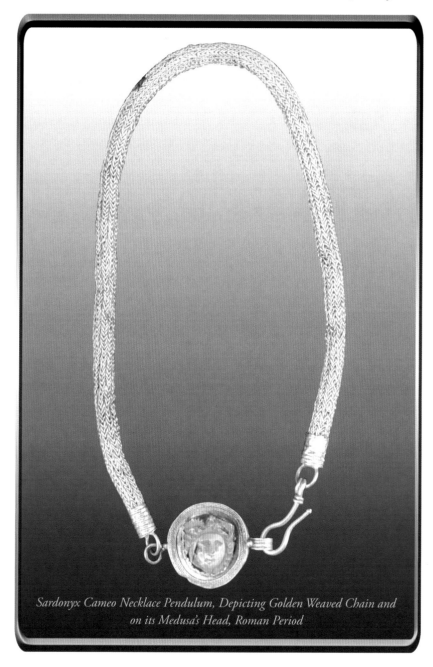

Sardonyx Cameo Necklace Pendulum, Depicting Golden Weaved Chain and on its Medusa's Head, Roman Period

From the Hellenistic Period onwards there was a rapid change in the jeweller's art. Alexander the Great's Asian campaign extended his empire's border as far as India, which had a positive influence in terms of both manufacturing techniques and increasing the range of themes is the jeweller's repertoire. Jewellery was no longer made from metals alone but was adorned with precious stones. New favoured depictions included the Maennad and Eros, portrayals of black people, and animal heads, particulary of lions, deer and bulls. Animal heads and composite depictions were especially popular in the eastern Mediterranean region.

Gold Earring with Eros Pendulum,
Hellenistic Period

The Roman world remained faithful to the artistic traditions of the preceding Hellenistic Period. Gold, silver and ivory were much used for personal adornment and semi-precious stones such as carnelian, amethyst, jasper, agate, garnet, sard and sardonyx as well as pearl and glass are commonly found in jewellery of the period.

Sardonyx Cameo Gold Earings, Depicting
Eros and Medusa, Roman Period

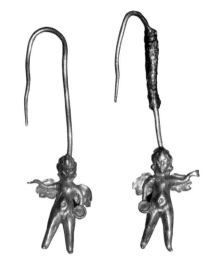

Glass came to be extensively used not only for making vessels but also for jewellery components on necklaces and rings as soon as large-scale, low cost glass production became feasible with the discovery of the blowpipe manufacturing technique in Syria in the middle of first century BC.

A Pair of Gold Earrings with Eros Pendulum,
Hellenistic Period

There are many extant examples of a wide range of Roman jewellery, including earrings, necklaces, finger rings and bracelets because jewellery was customarily deposited as offerings in burials and thereby survived to be discovered by excavation.

Amphora-Shaped Earrings with Gold
and Quartz Stone, Roman Period

A Pair of Roman Gold Earrings

Gold and Green Glass Beaded Necklace with
Crescent-Shaped Pendulum (Lunula)

A Pair of Roman Gold Earrings

Silver Reliquary Box, Byzantine Period

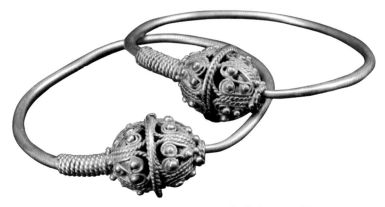

Gold Earrings, Byzantine Period, 4ʰ Century AD

In the Byzantine Period the influence of Christianity brought about distinct artistic changes in terms of both form and style and depictions were predominantly of Christian themes along with vegetal motifs. The tradition of placing gifts in burials was discontinued and this is one reason why fewer pieces of jewellery from this period have been discovered compared with those from earlier times.

Gold Earring with Pendulum in the Shape of a Cluster of Grapes, Roman Period

Gold Cross with Inscription of ΓΕΟΡΓΙΟC (Georgios), *Byzantine Period*

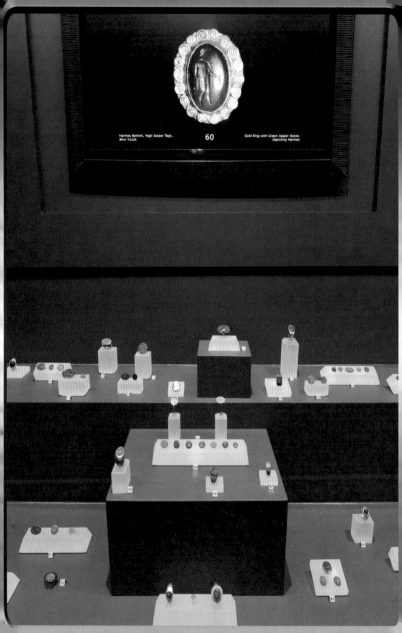

Hermes Betimli, Yeşil Jasper Taşlı,
Altın Yüzük

60

Gold Ring with Green Jasper Stone,
Depicting Hermes

Ringstones

Gemstones can be defined as precious or semi-precious of stone that are cut and polished to adorn lewellery or other objects. These stones are mostly cut by tools, either negatively (intaglio carving; counter-relief) or positively (cameo relief), commonly installed in the girdle of a finger-ring. They are also commonly found, in the form of larger relief stones, as part of necklace. Glass was used to imitiate the more expensive stones. Carved gemstones, which represent a significant

Gold Ring Depicting Persephone, 5ᵗʰ Century BC

Gold Ring with Carnelian Gem Depicting
Head of Diadumenos,
1ˢᵗ Century BC - 1ˢᵗ Century AD

portion of the present exhibit, had a practical use as official or personel seals. Furthermore, they were ornaments and some were used as amulets with healing and protective powers.

Gemstones had an aesthetic appeal as beautiful objects and as ornaments. Their actual function was as seals, being widely used to mark an invidual's property or demarcate a person's official capacities. A carved gemstone or a metal ring was impressed on a piece of clay or wax to make seals.

These types of seals could be easily broken and this would indicate if the envelope or object marked by the seal had been compromised.

The ring gemstones of the Greco-Roman period were mostly made from hard stones, quartz being the most common.

Gold Ring with Sard Gem Depicting Nike,
Roman Period

Gold Ring and Gem Depicting Horse, Roman Period

Cutting tools and techniques were selected according to the nature of the material to be worked. Pliny and Theophrastus briefly describe the methods used for carving and relief stone production. Our knowledge of these techniques is obtained by inference from modern methods and evidence from the ancient gemstones themselves.

The designs carved on ring gemstones reflected the fashion of the day. The most common motifs were picture-based. Copies of the statues of deities, portraits, images of heroes, animals, mythological scenes and creatures, objects, symbols and scenes from daily life were the prevalent depictions during the Roman period. Especially favoured themes included the deities worshipped by soldiers and traders, in particular Athena, Nike, Ares and Hermes. Official and private portraits were also widespread. Many stones extant today bear the portraits of Hellenistic kings and Roman emperors, which had an important propaganda value.

Carnelian Ring Stone, Depicting Nymphe's Head, Roman Period

Amethyst Ring Stone, Depicting Nymphe's Head, Roman Period

Black Sardonyx Ring Stone, Depicting Harpocrates, Roman Period

Green Jasper Ring Stone, Depicting Harpocrates, Roman Period

Animals as symbols were favoured in depictions. For example, the ram's head symbolised good fortune. The lion or the moon-with-star were symbols that evoked the deity Men-Mithras. The bee represented fertility and was the symbol of Artemis. Eagles were popular among legionary soldiers. However it is sometimes difficult to interpret a given motif because the meaning of some of the characters and objects is no longer apparent. Combinations of various figures, masks, animal parts and satyr heads, called grylloi (a misplaced term, since gryllos means caricature), became very popular from the 1st century BC onwards.

These were not merely figments of the imagination, but derived their significance from superstitions. They were used as amulets to protect against the evil eye or to ensure the owner's fertility or prosperity. Whereas it was fashionable in the Roman world to depict the portraits of the emperor and empress, Byzantine ring gemstones of the Early Christian Era emphasized religious motifs and it was common to inscribe personal names as monograms.

Rock Crystal Ring Stone, Depicting a Pheasant, Roman Period

The colours and characteristics of the stones varied and these dictated the employment of specific motifs. Presumably due to its natural colour, the lion's mane was usually shown on yellow jasper stones from the 2nd century AD onwards. Bloodstone and hematite were popular magical stones in Egypt, and the portrait of the sun god Helios was usually carved on bloodstone, which partly explains why this stone was called heliotrope in Greek. Many amethyst or similarly mauve-coloured glass stones have the mask of Dionysus carved on them, which makes for a striking combination: the image of the intoxicating Wine God on a stone that was believed to provide immunity to intoxication from alcohol (the name "amethyst" is derived from the Greek word "amethustos" meaning "not drunken").

Amethyst Ring Stone, Depicting an Emperor and Empress Bust, Roman Period

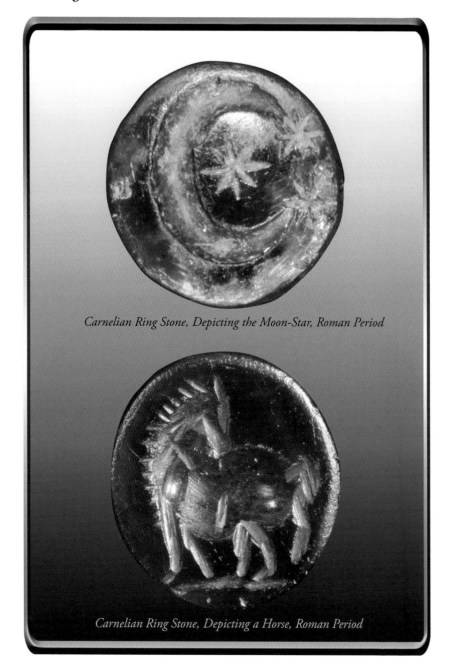

Carnelian Ring Stone, Depicting the Moon-Star, Roman Period

Carnelian Ring Stone, Depicting a Horse, Roman Period

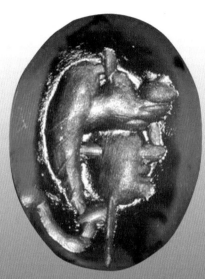

Carnelian Ring Stone, Depicting Grotesque Human Head, Roman Period

Carnelian Ring Stone, Depicting Ant, Roman Period

Yellow-Brown Jasper Ring Stone, Depicting the Lion Stepping on a Bull's Head and with an Inscription

Red Jasper Ring Stone, Depicting a Lion and the Moon-Star

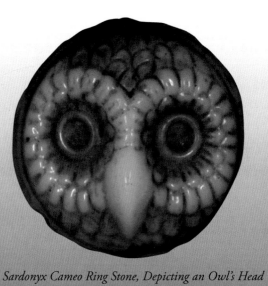

Sardonyx Cameo Ring Stone, Depicting an Owl's Head

Red Jasper Ring Stone, Depicting a Mountain Goat and Her Kid

Antique Coins

The purpose of exhibit is to present a series of coins based on the finest specimens from the Coin Cabinet of the Museum of Anatolian Civilizations. The exhibit begins with the first known coinage, that of kingdom of Lydia, and continues chronologically up to the final period of the Ottoman Empire.

What is a Coin?

A coin is a small piece of metal, of predetermined weight, that has on its surface an image, inscription, or some other mark, of the authority, state or person(s) producing it. Before the use of coins, various objects, grain commodities and livestock were used for barter in trade, eventually to be replaced by metal items with specific weights, a development transitional to the use coins. The first coins in the ancient world were made in the simple mints called ΑΡΓΥΡΟΚΟΠΕΙΟΝ (=ARGUROKOPEION). The molten metal was first moulded into a small disc, or blank, with a specific weight. The blank was then heated and placed between two dies, the bottom die being the anvil and the upper on the stamp. The upper die was then struck with a hammer in order to mint the coin.

Greek Coins (Display Case 11):

Included in the Greek Coins display-case are; examples from the very inventors of coinage, the Lydians, dating to the mid-seventh century BC; coins of the Archaic and Classical periods, which bear witness to the development of the plastic arts by the Greeks, who founded independent cities in Ionia; Satrapy coins from the Classical period (480-330 BC), and the coins of the Hellenistic kingdoms and cities founded in Anatolia after Alexander the Great. Brief information about these important periods, and the art and characteristics of their coins, is also presented.

1: *Electrum Stater. Kings of Lydia. Time of Alyattes-Kroisos. Circa 610-546 BC.*

2: *Electrum Stater. Mint of Kyzikos. Circa 475-460 BC.*

Depictions of animals and mythical creatures appear on coins of the Archaic period, with lion and bull protomes being especially popular. Later in the Archaic period, the figures and heads of gods and goddesses are shown, an indication of the importance of religion in ancient society. However, the images on the coins do not conform to the principles of true perspective. In profile views, for instance, eyes are depicted frontally. The reverse of the coins are generally concave.

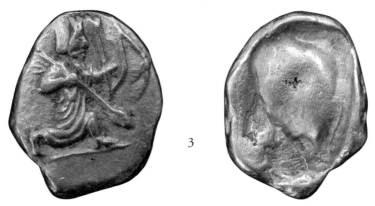

3

3 : *Persia. Achaemenid Empire. Mint of Sardes-Lydia. Time of Darios I to Xerxes II. Circa 485-420 BC. AV Stater or Daric.*

On the earliest coins of the Classical style, which reached its peak during the time between the Persian Wars and the reign of Alexander the Great, the cheerful smile of Archaic figures gives way to a noble and dignified sobriety. Harmony, balance and sobriety predominate in the Classical high style. Towards the end of the 5th century BC, however, this balanced sobriety disappears and there is an effort to attain exuberant figures fluid in movement. The tendency is towards elegance, beauty and a more realistic portraiture; figures are at the same time more naturally depicted and forms are softer, with compositions richer and more detailed. The art of the 4th century BC is more interested in human concerns and feelings. The individual and subjective ideals prevail. The expression of the inner world and pathos of the figures bring them liveliness and animation.

4 : *AR Stater. Mint of Aspendos-Pamphylia. 380-330 BC.*

5 : *AR Stater. Mint of Celenderis-Cilicia. 380-370 BC.*

6 : *King of Macedon. Antigonos III Doson (229-221 BC).*
AR Tetradrachm. Mint of Amphipolis.

7 : *AV Octodrachm. Seleucid Kingdom. Antiochus I Soter (281-261 BC).*

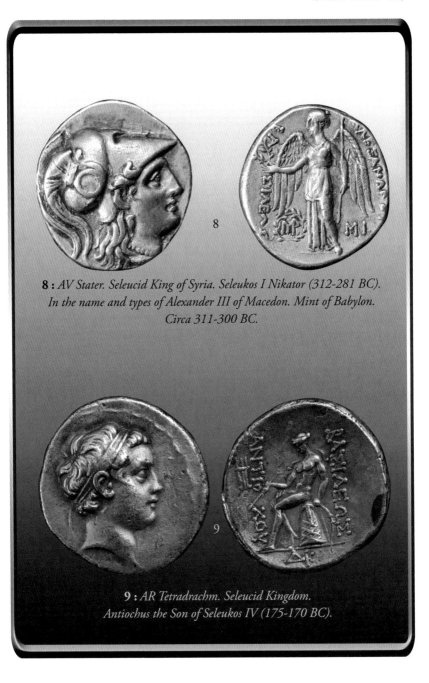

8 : *AV Stater. Seleucid King of Syria. Seleukos I Nikator (312-281 BC). In the name and types of Alexander III of Macedon. Mint of Babylon. Circa 311-300 BC.*

9 : *AR Tetradrachm. Seleucid Kingdom. Antiochus the Son of Seleukos IV (175-170 BC).*

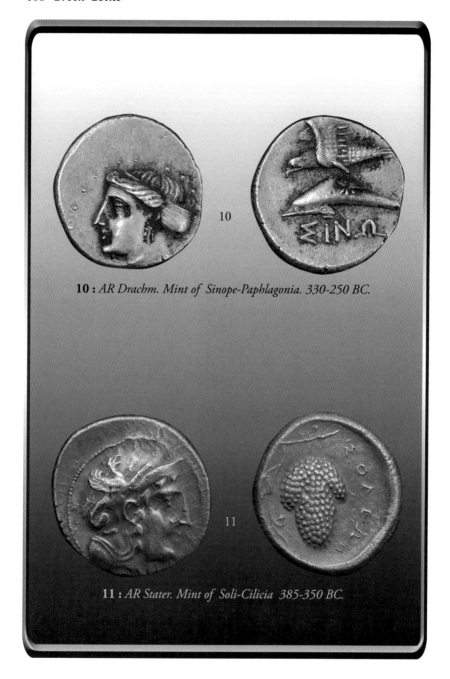

10 : *AR Drachm. Mint of Sinope-Paphlagonia. 330-250 BC.*

11 : *AR Stater. Mint of Soli-Cilicia 385-350 BC.*

The depiction of deities is of great importance on coins of the Classical period. In particular, the heads of gods and goddess are selected as appropriate motifs. The art is now freed from the conventions of the Archaic Period, and heads of gods are realistically depicted in profile.

In the 5th century BC, depictions resembling portraiture are rarely seen on coins. However, from the time of Alexander the Great onwards, portraiture became the most outstanding feature of Hellenistic art (330-30 BC), with a continuous series of incomparably fine royal portraits, and such is frequently seen on coins of the period. A great step towards the realistic portrait was taken with the coins depicting the young Alexander wearing the lion skin of Heracles, who was considered the legendary ancestor of the Macedonian kings and was believed to share the same facial features as Alexander. In the early Hellenistic Period, portraiture depicted the gods as human but with the lines of deified kings, and for this reason the depiction of the monarch on the obverse of the coins was still viewed as a divine image. Royal portraits on coins should thus be considered as religious images.

After Alexander, almost all of his successors, the Diodochs, struck coins bearing their names and actual portraits. The best examples are the coins from the kingdoms of Macedonia, Thrace, Pontus, Bithynia, Pergamum, Cappadocia, Seleucid Syria and the Ptolemaic dynasty in Egypt.

Roman Coins (Display Case 10):

Coinage developed differently in the Roman world. Even though the Greek colonies in southern Italy and Sicily minted coins from early on, Rome only produced its first national currency in the third century BC. The earliest examples, manufactured by the casting technique and named Aes Grave, were followed by the silver denarius that began circulation in the last quarter of the third century BC. The silver denarius was Rome's best known form of currency.

1 : *AR Denarius. L. FURIUS BROCCHUS. Mint of Rome. 63 BC.*

The first stage in the chronological development of Roman coinage was in the Republican Period, with the denarius as the basic unit. It was the imperial period, beginning with Emperor Augustus (27 BC-AD 14) and ending with Honorius (AD 395-423), that witnessed changes. The denarius maintained its significance until the reign of Emperor Caracalla. The Antoninianus coins, made of devalued silver, were introduced as a measure of austerity during the time of Emperor Caracalla. The denarius gradually and slowly went out of circulation. Gold and bronze coins were also minted alongside silver during the Imperial period. The early gold coinage, named aureus, was replaced by the solidus unit in the Late Roman period.

2 : *AR Denarius. Q. VOCONIUS VITULUS. Mint of Rome. 40 BC.*

3 : *AR Denarius. Q. SICINIUS. Mint of Rome. 49 BC.*

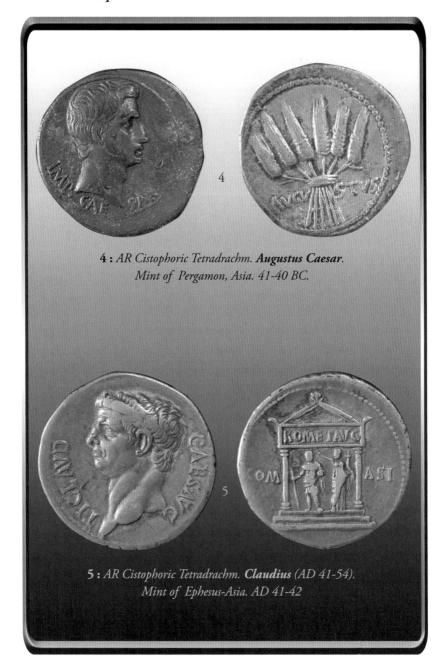

4 : *AR Cistophoric Tetradrachm.* **Augustus Caesar**.
Mint of Pergamon, Asia. 41-40 BC.

5 : *AR Cistophoric Tetradrachm.* **Claudius** *(AD 41-54).*
Mint of Ephesus-Asia. AD 41-42

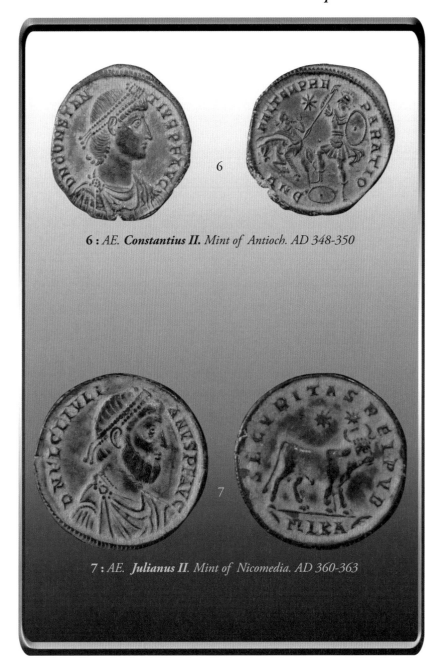

6 : *AE.* **Constantius II.** *Mint of Antioch. AD 348-350*

7 : *AE.* *Julianus II. Mint of Nicomedia. AD 360-363*

8 : *AV Solidus.* **Julianus II**. *Mint of Thessalonica. AD 360-363*

9 : *AV Solidus.* **Valens (AD 364-378)**. *Mint of Antioehia. AD 364-367*

10 : *AE 4 Assaria.* **Commodus (AD 180-192).** *Mint of Caesarea-Cappodocia.*

Exhibited in the section of the exhibition on Roman coins, the Roman Imperial Period coins (dating from 30 BC to AD 276) are a very important for the history of minting in Asia Minor. Due to local needs, even the smaller urban centres produced bronze coins. Approximately 350 Anatolian cities minted bronze coins during this period, with the permission of the Roman Emperors and the Roman Senate. Some important Anatolian cities were also given permission to mint silver coins (for example Amisus, Antiocheia, Ephesus, Caisareia and Tarsus). These civic coins had on the observe a life-like portrait of the reigning emperor, and on the reverse a number of figures and compositions reflecting the city's economic, social and religious life; as such they are vital sources for Anatolian history. These diverse coins were circulated in great quantities over very long periods of time, attesting to Anatolia's prosperity of the Pax Romana ("Roman Peace").

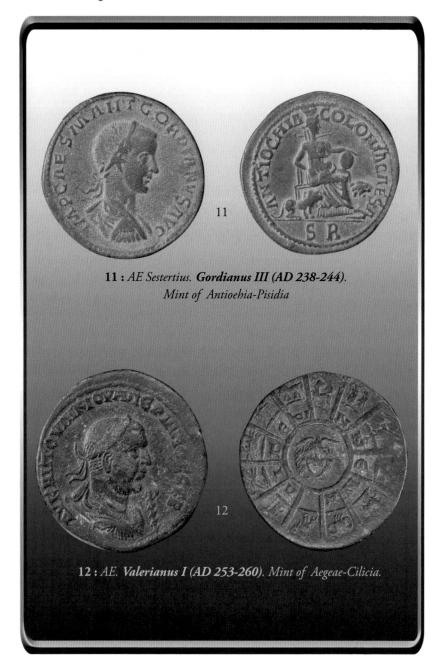

11 : *AE Sestertius.* **Gordianus III (AD 238-244).**
Mint of Antioehia-Pisidia

12 : *AE.* **Valerianus I (AD 253-260).** *Mint of Aegeae-Cilicia.*

13 : *AE.* ***Marcus Aurelius (AD 161-180).*** *Mint of Carrhae-Mesopotamia*

14 : *AE Medallion.* ***Caracalla (AD 198-217).*** *Mint of Pergamon.*

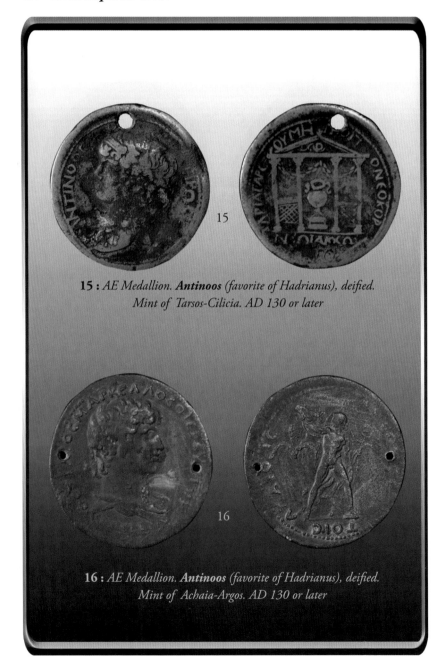

15 : *AE Medallion.* **Antinoos** *(favorite of Hadrianus), deified.*
Mint of Tarsos-Cilicia. AD 130 or later

16 : *AE Medallion.* **Antinoos** *(favorite of Hadrianus), deified.*
Mint of Achaia-Argos. AD 130 or later

17 : *AE Medallion.* **Trebonianus Gallus** *(AD 251-253).*
Mint of Rome

Byzantine Coins (Display Case 9):

The Roman Empire was divided into an eastern and western part after the death of the emperor Theodosius I in 395. The Eastern Roman Empire was left to Arcadius whereas Honorius was given the Western Roman Empire. Experts disagree on whether the production of Byzantine coins began under Emperor Arcadius or Anastasius. The Byzantine coins in the Museum's collection begin with those dated to the reign of Arcadius.

Byzantine coins were usually made of gold, electrum, silver and bronze. The decline in the Byzantine economy started in the 11th century and consequently the electron, made of low carat gold, came to be minted along with the low carat silver coin named the billion.

1 : *AE.* **Arcadius** *(AD 395-408)*

2

2 : *AE Follis.* ***Justinian I*** *(AD 527-565)*
Mint of Constantinople.

The gold coin, the solidus, was named nomisma by Byzantine writers; it was 24 carat gold until the end of the 11th century. The silver coin, named the hexagram, was minted during the reign of Emperor Heraclius. The concave or cup-shaped scyphate, a new type of coin, entered circulation during the time of Alexius I. Anastasius' coin reform in the fifth century AD is most evident with copper coins. The largest unit was the follis. Letters indicated values. For example, the capital letter M on the coin's reserve would indicate a specific value (M=40 nummi, K=20 nummi, I= 10, E=5 nummi).

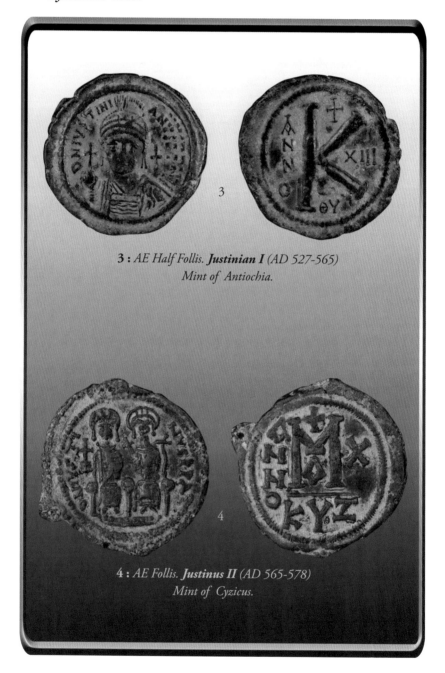

3 : *AE Half Follis.* **Justinian I** *(AD 527-565)*
Mint of Antiochia.

4 : *AE Follis.* **Justinus II** *(AD 565-578)*
Mint of Cyzicus.

5 : *AR Miliaresion.* **Romanus III** *(AD 1028-1034)*

Byzantine coins are typologically very different from those of the Roman period. The images of Byzantine coin iconography were not realistic portraits. During the time of Justinianus I (527-565 AD), portraits became frontally depicted. Initially only the emperor was shown on coins but in time other members of the royal family came to be included. Two or three full-sized figures can appear on the obverse. Coins began depicting Jesus during the reign of Justinianus II, and Virgin Mary during the time of Leo IV. There are also changes in the use of titles. For example, the royal title AVGVSTVS was replaced by ΒΑΣΙΛΕΩΣ (=BASILEOS) ("king").

Byzantine coins were produced at approximately 30 mints. The marks of these mints can be detected on the coinage until the eight century AD.

6 : *AV Solidius. Theodosius II (AD 408-450)*
Mint of Constantinople

7 : *AR Miliaresion.* **Constantine X** *(AD 1059-1067)*

8 : *AR Miliaresion.* **Basil II** *(AD 976-1025)*

9 : *AV Solidius.* **Basileus I** *(AD 867-886)*

Islamic Coins (Display Case 8):

Chronologically, the next coins in the exhibit are those belonging to the Seljuks in Anatolia, after the Byzantine Empire, followed by the coins of the various principalities that emerged after the downfall of the Seljuks. Finally, there are coins from the Ottoman Empire, dating from the time of its foundation in 1299 until its end in 1923.

Islamic coins are characterised in particular by the Arabic inscriptions embellishing them.

The first Islamic coin was minted year 76 of the Hijri (i.e Muslims) calendar (i.e AD 698), by the Umayyad Caliph Abdul Malik Bin Marwan. The minting of coins was, along with the mention of the ruler's name in public religious sermons, a prerogative of sovereignty in the Islamic world. Islamic coins were universally imprinted with prayers in the Arabic script, as well as geometric and vegetal ornamentation. Figurative elements were rare. The units for these coins were the gold dinar (denarius), the silver dirham (drahmi), and the copper fels (follis).

1

1 : *AR Drachm. **Arab-Sasanian. In the name of el-Haccac b. Yusuf**.*
71 H (AD 690)

2 : *AR Drachm.* **Ghiyath al-Din Kaykhusraw II** *634-643 H (AD 1236-1245).*
The Rum Seljuk of Central Anatolia.

The Umayyads, the Abbasids, the Fatimids, the Ayyubids, the Mamluk, the Seljuks and the Ottomans, as well as other Islamic states such as the Ikhshidids, Khwarazmians, Samanids, Safavids, Akkoyunlu and Karakoyunlu all minted coins.

Tuğrul Bey (1040-1157) was the first ruler of the Great Seljuk Empire to mint coins. The Turks migrated from Central Asia in waves and settled in Anatolia, becoming part of the cultural mosaic of Anatolian civilizations. These political developments are very finely attested in the coinage of the Danishmends, Mengujekids, Saltukids, Artuqids, Zengids, Inalids, and Ermenshahs, all principalities found in Anatolia. Both sides of some of these coins were minted in Byzantine style. Others bore Arabic inscriptions on the reserve. The Anatolian Seljuks first minted gold and silver coins under Kılıçarslan II. The cavalry was an image often used on Seljuk copper coins. Of great interest are the silver coins minted by Giyaseddin Keyhüsrev II (Ghiyath Al-Din Kaykhusraw II) in the name of his spouse, Tamara, who was Georgian. On these silver coins one finds the depiction known as the Şir-i Hurşit (Lion and

Sun), the "Lion" representing the king and the "Sun" representing the Georgian princess.

The Ilkhanates, who ruled Anatolia 14th century, minted coins employing both Arabic script and Mongolian. This was a novelty.

The first coinage of the Ottoman state was minted under Osman Bey (1299-1324), the founder of the state. Ottoman silver coins were named "akçe" (read: "akche"), meaning "white coin" in Mongolian. The first silver coinage was minted under Orhan Bey and the first gold coinage under Sultan Mehmed the Conqueror. The largest quantity of gold coins was minted under Sultan Suleiman the Magnificent. The first nickel money was introduced under Mehmet Reşat V.

In 1840, the first paper money was printed during the reign of Sultan Abdülmecit (Abd al-Majid). It was in use until the time of Mehmet Vahdettin, the last monarch of the Ottoman Empire.

3

3 : *AE Dirhem.* **Najm al-Din Alpi.**
547-572 H (AD 1152-1176)

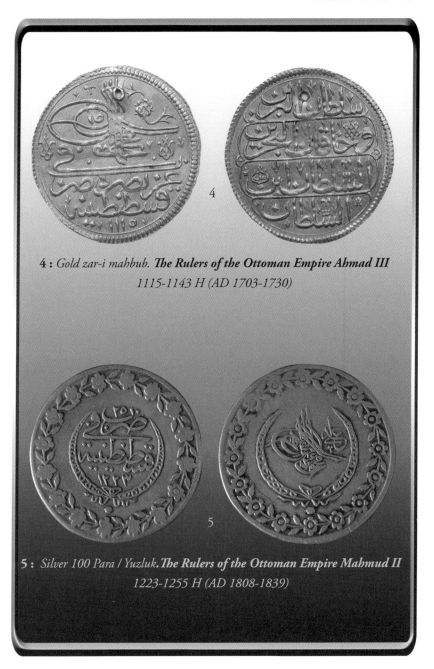

4 : *Gold zar-i mahbub. The Rulers of the Ottoman Empire Ahmad III 1115-1143 H (AD 1703-1730)*

5 : *Silver 100 Para / Yuzluk. The Rulers of the Ottoman Empire Mahmud II 1223-1255 H (AD 1808-1839)*

6 : *Gold-Silver-Red Enamel. **The Rulers of the Ottoman Empire Abd al-Majid** 1255-1277 H (AD 1839-1861)*

7 : *Silver-Green Enamel. The Rulers of the Ottoman Empire Abdül-Azîz*
1277-1293 H (AD 1861-1876)

The Sculpture of
Ancient Greece and
Rome

Sculptures in ancient Greek culture were first produced for the house of god, i.e. the temple and the cult statue. According to extant evidence, marble sculptures were not produced in Greek art until the mid 7th century BC, but it is a common belief that it appeared as an outcome of commercial relations with the East. In Greek art, this period is known as the "Archaic Period" (660-480/470).

At the end of the Archaic Period, progress was made in solving anatomical problems. From the second quarter of the 5th century BC onwards, earlier experience in Greek art culminated in the perfection of artworks. In the study of Greek sculpture, this period is known as the "Classical Period" (480-330 BC). The changing social life and new approaches were accompanied with the abandonment of the Archaic style, the making of statues of individuals to immortalize heroes, and the interest in depicting the gods not just with their symbols but also their characteristic facial features. The depiction of the human body became very important in the Classical Period. The impact of Classical Period sculpture was felt on both sides of the Aegean, whereas an established traditional style persisted in Anatolia.

Alexander the Great, king of Macedonia, ruled between 334-232 BC and conquered mainland Greece, Anatolia, the domains of the Persian Empire, and Egypt. He founded an empire with borders extending as far as India. This period, known as the "Hellenistic Period" (330-30 BC), was a time of novelty for the art of sculpture. The democratization in the Hellenistic Period resulted in the emergence of independent works of art in architecture and sculpture. With the changing climate of thought, Hellenistic society reformulated the art of sculpture with innovations not seen in the Classical period. While the approach in the Classical period was the search for idealism and the emphasis on beauty, the Hellenistic period produced more realistic sculpture in harmony with the new way of thinking. In depictions of ordinary citizens, reality was transmitted to the sculpture with all its bareness and naturalism.

Head of Persian Man, Late 6ᵗʰ Century BC

Head of a Woman, Late Hellenistic Period

Portrait of Empress Livia, August Period, 14 BC - AD 37

Portrait of a Man, Hellenistic Period

Portrait of a Administrator, Roman Republician Period, 1ˢᵗ Century BC

Display Case 13

Head of a Young Athlete, Roman Period

Head of a Young Woman (or Aphrodite ?), Roman Period

In this period, the "Pergamon School" was the foremost amongst others in the art of sculpture. One of its prominent features is how brilliantly Pergamon artwork expresses physical dynamism with stable expressions. The Great Altar of Zeus, presently displayed at the Pergamon Museum in Berlin, is of utmost importance for showing the high level attained by the "Pergamon School".

Statuette of a Man, Roman Period

Head of a Young Athlete, Roman Period

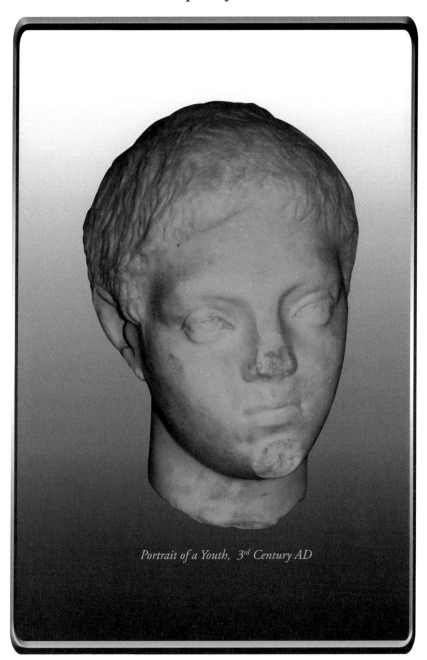

Portrait of a Youth, 3ʳᵈ Century AD

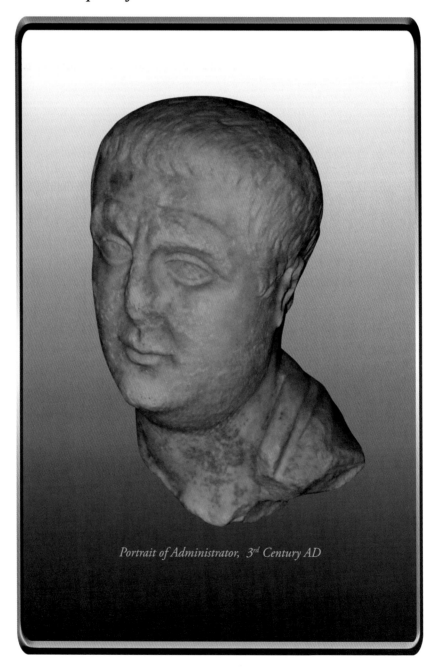

Portrait of Administrator, 3rd Century AD

In the Roman period, the art of sculpture was well developed and played an important role in copying the masterpieces produced in the Classical and Hellenistic periods and thus constituting an archive for the present.

In Roman art, progression of realism can be considered as characteristic of this period. In Roman cities, sculptures and busts of men and women were set up in public buildings, private houses and graves. These portraits, which reflected the physical features and personal characteristics of the models, became leading examples in Roman art.

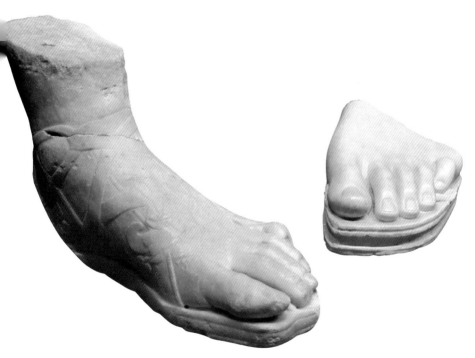

Foot Shaped Sculpture (Votive use?), Roman Period

Display Case 14

Statuette of Asklepios, Roman Period

The portraits of the Roman Republic period (509-27 BC) were usually set up by the Senate for politicians and military commanders following a military success. In the Roman Imperial period (27 BC-476 AD), this art was used to honour the emperor and his family in Rome and in the provinces as a vehicle of propaganda to recognize the political and military tutelage of Rome.

Statuette of Lying Eros, Roman Period

Undoubtedly the most important Roman portraits are the official portraits of the Roman Emperors. These imperial portraits were manufactured in Rome and sent to the provinces as an instrument of policy for the particular region. At the same time, these prototypes were multiplied by local workshops. Other than the emperors, the portraits of women, adolescents, children and priests, Roman elites, philosophers and writers were also made reflecting their personal attributes.

Statuette of Hygieia, Roman Period

Bust of God Men, Roman Period

Statuette of Tyche, Roman Period

Display Case 15

Statuette of God Helios (Helios-Mithras?), Roman Period

Although in Anatolia prominent workshops in Pergamon, Ephesus, Aphrodisias and Perge apparently depended on Rome, they nevertheless adhered to their own style and traditions, and continued to manufacture during the Roman Imperial period with great success.

Head of Hekate, Roman Period

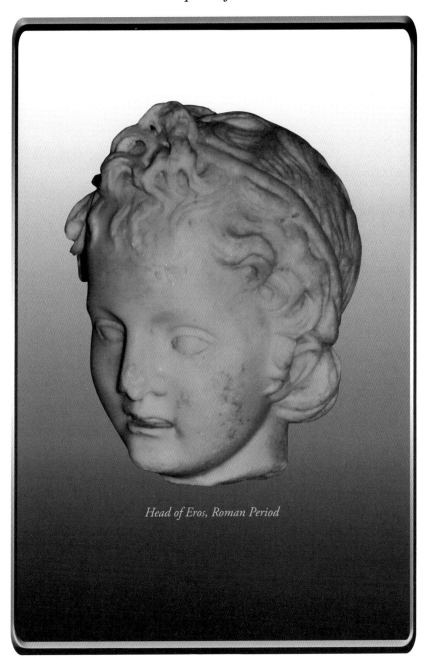

Head of Eros, Roman Period

Statuette of Eros, Roman Period

Statuette of Hygieia, Roman Period

14-15 **Korinth Aryballos,** M.Ö. 6. Yüzyıl
A Corinthian Aryballos, 6ᵗʰ Century B.C.

16 **Frig Tulum Formlu Kap,** M.Ö. 7-6. Yüzyıl
A Phrygian Form of Animal Skin Cup, 6ᵗʰ Century B.C.

17 **Attika Kırmızı Figür Çan Krater,** M.Ö. 5. Yüzyıl
An Attic Red-Figure Bell-Krater, 5ᵗʰ Century B.C.

18 **Attika Siyah Figür Oinochoe,** M.Ö. 5. Yüzyıl
An Attic Black-Figure Oinochoe, 5ᵗʰ Century B.C.

19-20 **Attika Kırmızı Figür Bodur Lekythos,** M.Ö. 5. Yüzyıl
An Attic Red-Figure Squat Lekythos, 5ᵗʰ Century B.C.

21 **Attika Kırmızı Figür Lebes Gamikos,** M.Ö. 5. Yüzyıl
An Attic Red-Figure Lebes Gamikos, 5ᵗʰ Century B.C.

22 **Attika Siyah Figür Skyphos,** M.Ö. 5. Yüzyıl
An Attic Black-Figure Skyphos, 5ᵗʰ Century B.C.

23 **Attika Kırmızı Figür Pelike,** M.Ö. 5. Yüzyıl
An Attic Red-Figure Pelike, 5ᵗʰ Century B.C.

24 **Attika Siyah Firnisli Kantharos,** M.Ö. 4. Yüzyıl
An Attic Black-glazed Kantharos, 4ᵗʰ Century B.C.

25 **Attika Kadın Büstü Lekythos,** M.Ö. 5. Yüzyıl
A Woman Bust Shaped Attic Lekythos, 5ᵗʰ Century B.C.

26 **Attika Kırmızı Figür Bodur Lekythos,** M.Ö. 5. Yüzyıl
An Attic Red-Figure Squat Lekythos, 5ᵗʰ Century B.C.

27 **Attika Squat Lekythos,** M.Ö. 5. Yüzyıl
An Attic Squat Lekythos, 5ᵗʰ Century B.C.

28 **Attika Alabastron,** M.Ö. 5. Yüzyıl
An Attic Alabastron, 5ᵗʰ Century B.C.

29-31 **Attika Siyah Figür Lekythos,** M.Ö. 5. Yüzyıl
An Attic Black-Figure Lekythos,

32 **Attika Siyah Firnisli Skyphos,** M.
An Attic Black-glazed Skyphos,

33 **Attika Siyah Firnisli Kantharos,**
An Attic Black-glazed Kantharos

Display Case 16

Anatolian
Pottery I

Anatolian Pottery
From the 1st Millennium BC to the Roman Period

The monochrome gray pottery dominating western Anatolia in the 1st millennium BC and the Protogeometric vessels uncovered at Bayraklı and Miletos comprise the earliest ceramic finds pertaining to their type of pottery. There is an increase in the number of ceramic samples during the end of the Geometric period and the Subgeometric phase.

A Lydian Pottery with Four Loop Handles,
7th-6th Centuries BC

A Lydian Stemmed Bowl,
7th - 6th Centuries BC

A Phrygian Pottery Mug,
8th - 7th Centuries BC

The earliest stage of the Geometric style ceramic samples found at centers in the regions of Ionia and Caria attest to black-painted vessel surfaces divided into metopes. The improvements concerning ceramics in the 8th century BC resulted in the drawing of animal and human figures with silhouette and shadow techniques. The meander, combed triangles, series of diamonds, and swastikas were also popular motifs.

A Lydian Pottery Earthen Pot,
7th - 6th Centuries BC

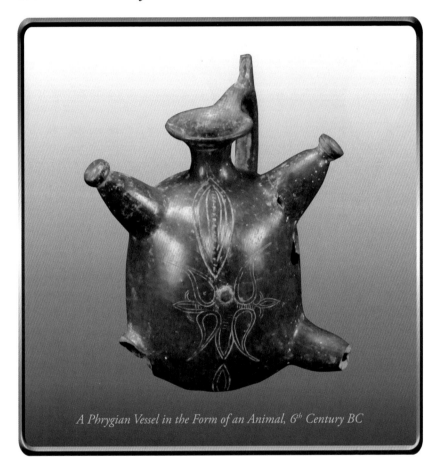

A Phrygian Vessel in the Form of an Animal, 6ᵗʰ Century BC

The period of the Orientalizing style (720-640 BC) was a transition between the Geometric and Archaic periods. The eastern influences on western Anatolian and Greek artists can be observed in ceramics. The straight and angled lines that characterize the designs of Geometric vessels are replaced by animal figures such as the lion or sphinx, and by plant motifs such as the lotus-palmette or the tree of life.

The Phrygians in central Anatolia during the 1st millennium BC used handmade ware ceramics designed with simple bands and lines in the Early Iron Age. In the Early-Middle Phrygian period (950-550 BC), designs were painted on a buff coloured, cream and beige slipped surface, and included triangular lozenges (strip), as well as cage, line and geometrical motifs like zig-zags which were very popular. Gray and black-slipped pottery decorated with lion and ram motifs was also used extensively. Filter vessels that were used for drinking beer were particularly popular.

An Attic Black - Glazed Kyathos, 4th Century BC

An Attic Red-Figure Oinochoe, 5ᵗʰ Century BC.

An Attic Red-Figure Pelike, 5ᵗʰ Century BC.

An Attic Red-Figure Squat Lekythos, 5th Century BC.

An Attic Red-Figure Lebes Gamikos,
5ᵗʰ Century BC

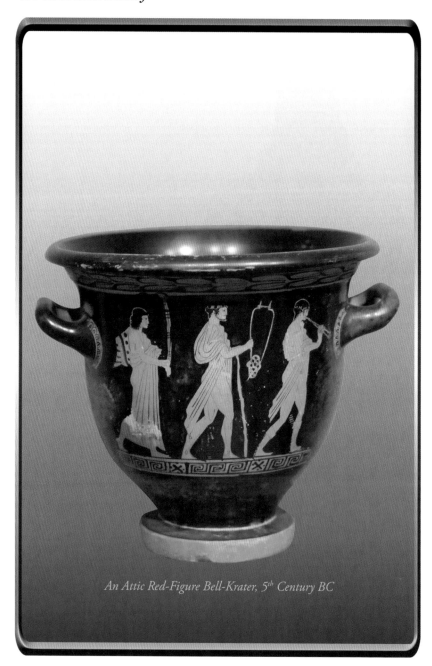

An Attic Red-Figure Bell-Krater, 5th Century BC

An Attic Black-glazed Skyphos (Kotyle), 4ᵗʰ Century BC

Anatolian
Pottery II

An Attic Black-glazed Hydria, 4ᵗʰ Century BC.

An Attic Black-glazed Kantharos, 4ᵗʰ Century BC

Hellenistic Double Handled Vessel, 2ⁿᵈ - 1ˢᵗ Centuries BC

Hellenistic Amphora, 3ʳᵈ Century BC

Galatian Pottery Oinochoe, 3rd - 2nd Centuries BC

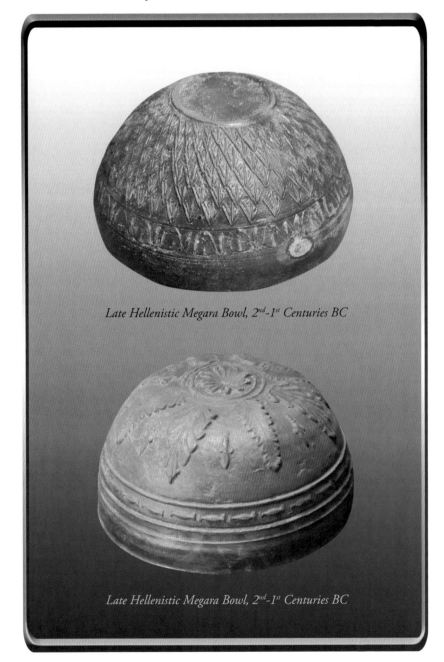

Late Hellenistic Megara Bowl, 2nd-1st Centuries BC

Late Hellenistic Megara Bowl, 2nd-1st Centuries BC

Early Roman Black-Ware Plate, circa 1ˢᵗ Centuries BC / AD

Early Roman Black-Ware Plate, circa 1ˢᵗ Centuries BC / AD

Vases painted with the black figure technique, produced in the Corinth workshop in Greece, made their appearance in the Archaic Period (650-480 BC). The figures were painted in black on a light red or orange surface, creating the effect of a silhouette. In addition to this technique that was used until the middle of the 5th century BC, vase painters began to use the red figure technique in the middle of the 6th century BC. In contrast to the black figure technique, figures were the colour of clay while the empty areas on the surface of the vase were painted with a black metallic colour.

Early Roman Lead-Glazed Skyphos, circa 1st Century BC / AD

Both techniques were used by Attic vase painters, showing mythological scenes or themes from daily life.

The Hellenistic period (330-30 BC) began with the conquests of Alexander the Great and continued until the founding of the Roman Empire. In this period, red and black figured vases were replaced by pottery that was covered with white slip and decorated with colours.

During this period in Anatolia, in eastern Phrygia, the Galatians produced red and pink coloured ceramics on a cream slip. The surfaces of this pottery were designed with plant and animal motifs. Ceramics from this region are called "Galatian" or "Kızılırmak Basin Pottery" because they are found within the region defined by the curve of the Kızılırmak River.

Bowls with reliefs from the city of Megara in Sicily during the Hellenistic period are referred to as "Megarian Bowls". They were also produced in the pottery workshops at Pergamum and were widely used in Anatolia. At the beginning of the Roman period, "Megarian Bowls" continued to be produced and used. During the Roman Empire period the most popular pottery was red-coloured, including relief-figured bowls known as "Terra Sigillata". In addition to red-painted pottery, domestically produced black and gray painted pottery was also fashionable.

A Roman Flask in the Form of a Man's Head,
2ⁿᵈ-1ˢᵗ Centuries BC

Display Case 18

Terracotta
Figurines in
Anatolia

The term "terracotta" generally refers to baked earth figurines but it also covers architectural elements. The tradition of manufacturing terracotta figurines in Anatolia goes back to the beginning of the Neolithic period. Initially, figurines were produced in a limited number for religious purposes but later this craft was transformed into a sector. An outcome of the-then emerging new techniques, a great number of figurines were obtained from temples, houses and graveyards. Differentiated from

Terracotta Figure Head of Bull, 2nd Millenium BC

the craftsmen who made pottery, the craftsmen who manufactured terracotta figurines were named the "coroplasts". The manufacture of terracotta figurines began in the Neolithic period and carried on in the same workshops that made the ceramic pottery in the first millennium BC, especially until the 6th century BC. After this period, they were mass produced in independent workshops and their numbers increased in sacred areas, cemeteries, and houses.

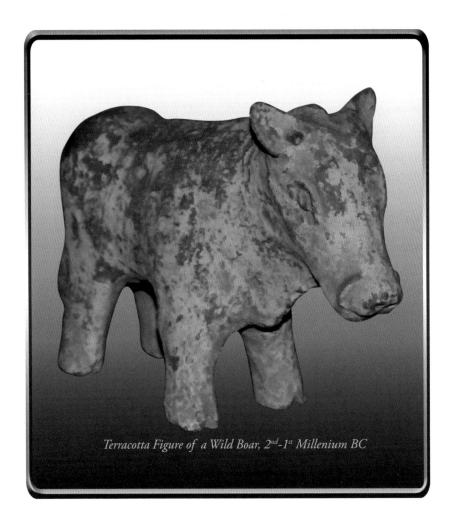

Terracotta Figure of a Wild Boar, 2nd-1st Millenium BC

Lydian Terracotta Architectural Fragment with Relief Head of Medusa,
7ᵗʰ-6ᵗʰ Centuries BC

The main material of the terracotta figures is clay. The quality of this material was improved by leaving it in pools after demanding and tough work in the kilns. Formerly they were made by hand but wheels were also used from the second half of the second millennium BC onwards. The lower parts of the figurines were made by using the wheel and upper body parts were shaped by hand. In later times, they were manufactured by using moulds. This technique offered the advantage of mass production.

At first, carved wooden models were prepared to obtain terracotta moulds which were fired at high temperatures around 1200 degrees. These terracotta moulds were then filled with milled clay and the front and back parts of the mould were joined together. The back of the moulds were drilled with circular or oval steam holes to avoid damage during firing. In the Roman period, plaster moulds were also used alongside terracotta moulds.

Terracotta Ryton of a Horse,
6th-5th Centuries BC

Terracotta figurines modeled by employing various techniques were covered with white clay before firing to make a slip. Subsequently details of garments, hair and features of the face were painted with various colours on the slip.

At the beginning, a limited number of figurines were produced as cult objects but in the 6th century BC, the use of mould techniques enabled the manufacture of great numbers of terracotta figurines in various contexts. Gods, goddesses, and mythological characters were made along with miniature copies of large scale sculptures. Various types of animal figurines, comical and caricature-like figures, grotesques, masks, statuettes with moving arms that could be dressed as the priestess of a worshipped goddess, figures of people from all the different social strata such as peasants, citizens, and soldiers, children's toys, and even rattles, became items of terracotta figure manufacture parallel to the developments of and changes in Hellenistic period art.

Terracotta Ryton of a Bull,
6th-5th Centuries BC

Syrian Terracotta Statuette of Astarte, 6th Century BC

The tradition and industry of terracotta figurines prospered during the Roman period until the 3rd century AD after which it lost its former importance and power.

Terracotta Architectural Fragment Figure of a Female,
5th-4th Centuries BC

A Flask in the Form of a Woman (or Persephone) Holding a Bird,
5ᵗʰ-4ᵗʰ Centuries BC"

Terracotta Statuette of Seated Kybele, 5th-4th Centuries BC

Classical Period Terracotta Figure of Woman Hydrophoros, 4ᵗʰ Century BC

Persian Terracotta Statuette of Horse and Riders, 4ᵗʰ Century BC

Terracotta Figure of Seated Eros Holding a Bird, 2nd - 1st Centuries BC

Terracotta Figure of Eros Holding a Goose, 2nd - 1st Centuries BC

Terracotta Statuette of a Woman, 3rd - 2nd Centuries BC

Terracotta Statuette of Aphrodite, 2ⁿᵈ - 1ˢᵗ Centuries BC

Terracotta Statuette of Woman (or Aphrodite), 3rd - 2nd Centuries BC

Byzantine Terracotta Head of a Woman (or Empress ?)
5th - 6th Centuries AD

Bronze Statue of Dionysos, Roman Period

A Roman Bronze Statue of Dionysos, 1ˢᵗ Century AD

A Roman Marble Statue of Athena, 2ⁿᵈ Century AD

The Funerary Stela of Gladiator Chrisampelos, Marble, Roman period, 2ⁿᵈ Century AD

Roman Limestone Ostothek, 1ˢᵗ-2ⁿᵈ Centuries AD

Osthotek, Limestone, Roman Period

Marble Statue of Hygieia, Roman Period

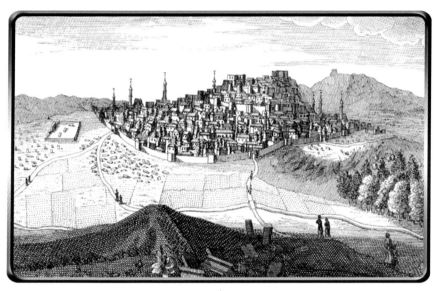

The City of Ankara in the 17ᵗʰ Century as seen on a Gravure

An Anonymous Oil Painting of Ankara in the 17ᵗʰ century. Rijks Museum, Amsterdam

The entrance of the Museum of Anatolian Civilizations